XO 5/11 (c. 2010)
GX 7/10 (9/14)

CHANGES

Going to the Hospital

By Janine Amos

Photographs by Howard Davies

alphabet
SOUP

an imprint of
WINDMILL BOOKS
New York

Published in the United States by Alphabet Soup, an imprint of Windmill Books, LLC

Windmill Books
303 Park Avenue South
Suite #1280
New York, NY 10010

Library of Congress Cataloging-in-Publication Data

Amos, Janine
        Going to the hospital. – 1st North American ed. / by Janine Amos ; photographs by
Howard Davies.
                p.   cm. – (Changes)
        Includes bibliographical references and index.
        Summary: Letters, stories, and informational text explain what to expect
when you have to go to the hospital.
        ISBN 978-1-60754-484-5 (lib.) – ISBN 978-1-60754-486-9 (pbk.)
ISBN 978-1-60754-485-2 (6-pack)
        1. Hospitals—Juvenile literature   2. Hospital care—Juvenile literature
[1. Hospitals   2. Medical care]   I. Davies, Howard   II. Title   III. Series
        362.1/1—dc22

Manufactured in China

With thanks to our models: Jay Vachhani, Cameron Huggins, Bindu Patel, Oscar O'Brien, Georgia
Apsion, Kim Shaw, Eve-Marie Johnson, Sian Webber, Molly Mitton, Tilly Tappenden, Elise Brack, Becky
Clark, Lily Reddaway, Lynne Ridden, Jack Harper, Dominic Bentley, Christine Harper and Max
Chandler. With special thanks to Rachel Clinton, Mark Taylor, Kim Bromwich, Leanne Privett and
Catherine Tatum at the Royal Alexandra Children's Hospital.

Contents

Letters:
  Dear Charlie ... Dear Jay   4
Story:
  What's the matter?   6
Letters:
  Dear Aunt Jan ... Dear Grace   12
Going to the Hospital   14
Getting Ready to Go In   16
Letters:
  Dear Charlie ... Jay's Hospital Diary   18
Feelings in the Hospital   20
Helping Yourself in the Hospital   22
Story:
  Freya's Birthday   24
Letters:
  Dear Aunt Jan ... Dear Grace   30
Glossary   32
Index   32
For Further Reading   32
Web Sites   32

Dear Charlie,

Here I am in the hospital, waiting for my operation. It's tomorrow morning, really early, so I'm sleeping here tonight. I thought I'd write you a letter as I promised.

When I got here it felt a bit scary. There are loads of people and everyone's busy. It felt strange to know that I'm going to sleep here. I thought I'd have to put my pajamas on and get into bed. My nurse is named Kim. She's fun. She told me I could stay in my tracksuit. Then she showed me the green gowns and masks the doctors will wear tomorrow for my operation (just like on TV). She told me exactly what will happen to me. I don't feel so worried now.

I have to have an injection before the operation. I told Kim I really hate shots. She says they'll put some special cream on my hand so it goes numb. Then I'll only feel a tiny prick. I met the doctor too. She prodded my stomach and told me a Knock Knock joke.

The main thing I'm worried about is that I won't be able to go skiing with you after Christmas. I'm scared to ask in case they say no.

Your friend, Jay

p.s. There's a boy here named George. We're going to play a game of cards before we watch TV.

4

Dear Jay,

It sounds like hospital's OK. If you're still there next Saturday, Mom's promised to drive us over to see you. She says Children's Wards don't have special visiting times — so we can stay all day. We'll bring you your favorite chocolate cake. Yummy!

Your doctor sounds nice — why don't you just ask about skiing? It's better than worrying about it.

You'll have a new DVD to watch soon. Mom and I mailed it to the hospital with your name on it.

See you,

Charlie

What's the Matter?

Danny was in his room. His head ached. A fly buzzed at the window and the sun streamed in. Danny was hot and tired. He needed a drink.

Danny went to the kitchen, where his mom was chatting on the telephone. As soon as Danny came in, she quickly put down the phone.

"What's the matter?" asked Danny.

"Nothing, dear," said his mom, brightly.

"Something's going on," thought Danny.

The next morning Danny woke early. On his way to the bathroom, he passed his sister Emily's bedroom. She was still fast asleep. Danny tiptoed past. Then he heard voices from his mom and dad's room.

"I haven't said anything yet. We'll tell him nearer the time," his mom was saying. Something about his mom's voice made Danny stop and listen.

"He won't want to go, not our Dan. He'll make a fuss," replied Danny's dad.

"They're talking about me," thought Danny. "They're sending me away!"

Back in bed, Danny thought about his dad's words. Where wouldn't he want to go? And why were they sending him? His heart began to thump and he felt a bit sick. Had he done something wrong? All morning, Danny watched his mom. He helped her clean up after breakfast. He helped her wash the car.

When the telephone rang, Danny jumped.

"George's mother is on the phone," called Danny's mom. "Would you like to go there for lunch?"

Danny shook his head. He wanted to stay at home.

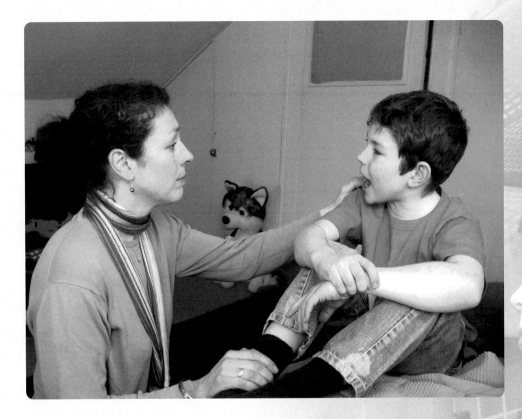

At suppertime, Danny couldn't eat. His headache was worse and he wanted to cry. It was awful, just waiting for something to happen. He went to his room and sat on his bed.

Just then, Danny's mom came in. "Is something the matter?" she asked.

Danny felt a wave of tears well up inside him. "You're sending me away!" he shouted. "I heard you!"

Danny's mom sat next to him on the bed. She gave Danny a big hug.

"Oh, I'm so sorry, Dan," she said. "I didn't mean to worry you."

Danny waited for his mom to continue. "You have to go to the hospital next week. You'll need to stay in for a few days. The doctors will do some checks on you. I'll be staying there with you."

"Who'll look after Emily?" asked Danny.

"Nana's coming," said his mom. "It's all arranged."

"Will you be with me all the time?" asked Danny.

"Yes," replied his mom. "And before then we'll visit the hospital together. You can see the Children's Ward and meet some of the nurses. Would you like that?"

Danny nodded.

At last the day came for Danny to go to the hospital. He packed a bag to take with him. He put in a pair of pajamas, a towel, two books, three comics, a photo of Button, his cat, and his old Teddy Bear.

"I don't mind about the hospital," said Danny as he and his mom left the house. "The thing I didn't like was not knowing."

"I understand that now," said Danny's mom slowly. "I got it wrong, didn't I?"

"That's okay," said Danny, smiling. "Let's go!"

Dear Aunt Jan,

Thanks for your card. Sorry about my writing — it's hard to write lying down! I've had the operation and I feel quite well, but I can't go home yet. I have to stay in bed. When I first got to the hospital I was checked by lots of doctors and nurses. They gave me X-rays and took blood tests. I couldn't have any breakfast before the operation. Afterward, I had lots of tubes in me. I wasn't scared because the nurses told me what they were all for and Mom slept on a cot next to me.

I thought it would be boring here but it's OK. The nurses are great and there are lots of other children. A teacher comes around every day with work for me. I still have to do maths, even in the hospital! We laughed. Yesterday I even made a cake lying down!

I'll be in here for a long time. I bet everyone at school will forget about me. Sammie will get to be Kim's best friend. They're doing a project together and working on it after school.

Please write soon.
Love, Grace xxx

Dear Grace,

It was great to get your letter. You sound as if you're doing really well in the hospital. I'll be in to see you next week.

Are you worried about what's going on at school while you're away? I remember feeling like that when I was sick and missed work. Is there anyone you can talk to about it — the teacher, a nurse, or your mom? They might have some ideas for keeping in touch with your friends at school. How about writing to Kim and the others?

I'll see you next week, Grace. If you do any more baking, keep a slice of cake for me!

Love, Aunt Jan xx

13

Going to the Hospital

When you first learn you'll have to go to the hospital you may feel worried. What will it be like?

■ It's natural to feel concerned about a new situation. If you are feeling nervous, talk about it with a grown-up. Together, try to work out what it is that worries you.

■ Some television programs about hospitals show frightening scenes of operations with lots of blood or big, beeping machines. You might remember these scenes whenever you think about hospitals. Don't forget, these scenes have nothing to do with you — and they're not real anyway! Hospital's simply a place for trying to make people better.

■ Some children may not like the thought of being away from home. They worry about sleeping in a strange bed without all their usual things around them.

■ Other children worry about leaving their pets behind. Will they be looked after properly?

Injections

Lots of people hate the idea of injections. If you're really worried, tell your parent and make sure the nurses know. A nurse will put some anesthetic cream on before the injection. It will make your skin numb so you won't feel the needle. Ask if you can play a story CD to take your mind off it. Don't look at the needle. Yell if you need to — but keep still. Remember, it will only prick for a few seconds.

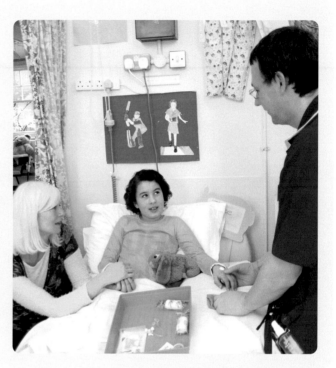

■ Friendships may worry you too. You might be scared that the friends in your class will forget about you, or that your best friend will start to like someone else more.

■ Sometimes, children wonder what they might be missing out on at school. Will they be able to catch up later?

Getting Ready to Go In

If you need to go to the hospital, there are some things you can do to prepare yourself.

■ Find out why you are going to the hospital and what will be done to you. Ask how long you will be there. If you don't understand everything, keep asking. If your parents have any questions, they can check with the hospital staff. Ask your parents if you can visit the hospital before you go in.

■ Share any worries with an adult. One of your parents can stay with you in the hospital. If they need to go home at any time, together find someone to be with you in their place.

■ If you have a pet, get someone in your family or a friend to look after it. Tell them your pet's likes and dislikes, so that you won't worry while you're away.

■ Ask if a school friend can visit you in the hospital. They'll keep you in touch with what's going on at school. Ask your teacher what the class will be doing while you're away. There might be some work you would like to do in hospital.

■ Pack a bag to take with you. You might like to pack (with your name on): your favorite toy; your favorite mug or drinking cup (even a bedtime bottle if you think it would help); writing things, books, small toys, games, DVDs; a bag with soap, a toothbrush, toothpaste, and a hairbrush; cool, light clothing (it's often hot in hospital!); two sets of pajamas.

Emergency

If you're rushed to the hospital in an emergency, you won't get time to prepare. There are some things you can do to help yourself cope. Take some deep breaths to help calm yourself. Remember, the nurses, doctors, and

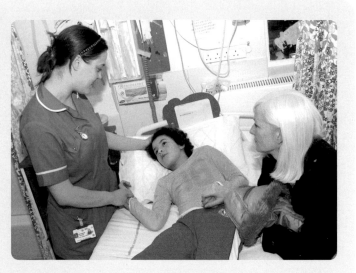

paramedics are doing their jobs as fast as they can to help you. Ask for someone to explain what's happening. Ask a nurse to hold your hand.

Dear Charlie,

Thanks for the DVD — it's great! I've watched it twice (the second time with George, the boy I met here).

I've had my operation and it was OK. I knew what was going on because the doctors and nurses talked to me all the time. Mom was with me and she asked some questions too. They made me go to sleep with an injection, so I didn't feel them doing the operation.

My stomach's a bit sore but the nurse said that will go after a few days. Mom is sleeping here at the hospital in a chair (it pulls out to make a bed). Dad's coming to see me after supper.

I'll be out by Saturday, so Mom says you can come to our house instead of the hospital (you can still bring the yummy cake).

I'm keeping a Hospital Diary of everything that happened while I was here. I can take it to school and show the class.

See you,
Jay

Hospital Diary

Monday
In Children's Ward. Mom and I met Kim the nurse. I went into the playroom and met a boy named George. Mom filled in a form. Kim checked my height, weight, and blood pressure. Ward is busy and noisy. Everyone is friendly. Won't be able to have breakfast tomorrow before my operation — so I stuffed myself at supper. Food here is OK.

Tuesday
Woke up early. Sign on my bed: NPO (it means I can't eat or drink until after the operation). They've just put cream on my hand and it is going numb, so I won't feel the injection.

Wednesday
My stomach is sore but Kim gives me medicine to make it feel better. Got up and went to see George. Don't remember much about yesterday. Worst bit was going into the anesthetic room. It was a bit scary then, but everyone was chatting and it was OK. Woke up and Mom was here. Had breakfast, lunch, and supper! Watched a new DVD from Aunt Cath and Charlie.

Thursday
Doctor says I'm fine. I can go home on Friday.

Thank you for looking after me. My stomach is fine now. Skiing is cool. I'm getting good.

Happy New Year to you all.
Love from
Jay Patel

The Children's Ward
Lowell Hospital
231 Oak Road
Lowell, MA 01855

19

Feelings in the Hospital

Hospitals are big, busy, noisy places. At first they may seem strange and a bit scary. There are unusual smells, lots of new people, large machines — everything is different from home or school.

■ Because the hospital is new to them and because everyone is so busy, some children feel small and powerless. They feel they can't ask questions. Never be afraid to ask.

■ Don't think your worries are silly. They are not. Some childen worry that their clothes will be taken away, that a strange nurse will bath them, that they'll be somehow different after their operation. These concerns are very real, so tell the nurse or doctor whatever your fears are.

■ For most children, the stay in hospital will be short. Others need to stay longer. Some quickly get used to hospital life, and may worry about leaving.

■ Other children get bored. They find it hard to read or do their schoolwork. They feel cut off from the real world and fed up with everything.

Operation

If you are to have an operation, these are the stages:

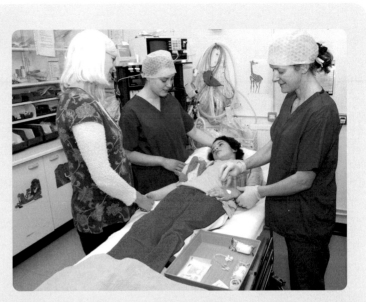

- Before the operation, you won't be able to eat or drink because you can't have an operation on a full stomach. You might change into a favorite T-shirt and some tracksuit bottoms.

- An hour before the operation, you may have some medicine. It will make you sleepy and your mouth will feel dry.

- You may have some cream put on your hand so that the needle for the anesthetic won't hurt.

- A nurse will take you and your parent to the anesthetic room to have the anesthetic. The anesthetic will make you sleep so you won't feel a thing.

- When you first wake up you'll be in the recovery room. Then you'll be wheeled back to the ward on a gurney. You might sleep for a long time. A nurse will bring you a drink.

- If you have any questions at all about your operation, just ask.

Helping Yourself in the Hospital

There are some things you can do to help yourself settle into the hospital. When you get to the ward, find some ways to make yourself feel more comfortable.

■ As soon as you can, learn your way around. Ask where the bathroom is. Find out what the times are for lunch and supper. Is there a playroom? If so, ask when you can visit it.

■

If you're going to have an operation, find out as much as you can about it. Ask a nurse to explain what will happen step by step.

■ Remember, all the people around you want to help you get better. Help them to help you by telling them how you feel. Don't keep any fears or worries to yourself. If you are staying in the hospital for a long time, you can help yourself in other ways too.

■ Keep in contact with friends at home and at school. Write them letters. Ask an adult to help you write a story about your hospital stay to send them.

■ Like Jay, keep a Hospital Diary. Write notes about what happens each day of your stay. Then you'll have your own hospital story to look back on when you're home again.

■ Keep as busy as you can. Ask your family if they'll bring in some different things to do. Swap games and DVDs with other children on the ward. Why not learn to do something new — how to braid your hair, play chess, or do painting-by-numbers?

■ Use your knowledge of hospital life to help someone else. Chat to the new children on the ward, tell them what goes on and help them to feel more confident. Ask a nurse or another adult if there's any other way you can help new patients to settle in.

Freya's Birthday

Freya sat up in bed. She threw down the book she'd been reading and sighed. A nurse went by and smiled at her. Freya didn't smile back.

Freya looked toward the door at the end of the Children's Ward. She could see her mom coming back with drinks from the machine. She closed her eyes and turned her face away.

"I've got some juice for you, Freya, and hot chocolate for myself. That coffee's awful!" murmured her mom.

Freya didn't want to answer. She felt angry with her mom. She felt angry with everyone. In two days it would be Freya's birthday. She'd be ten years old. And she was in the hospital.

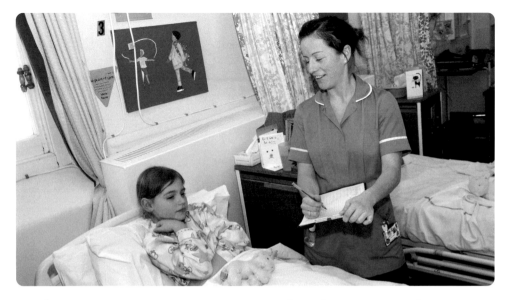

The next morning, Freya was woken by someone humming. A nurse was checking the charts at the end of her bed.

"Hi, I'm Leanne!" said the nurse.

Freya nodded.

"Wow," said Leanne. "You're a grouch. Is that tummy hurting you?"

"No," said Freya.

Leanne came to the side of the bed. "Your operation's all set for this afternoon. Any questions, I'm the one to ask. Okay?"

Leanne grinned and Freya gave her a wobbly smile.

Leanne looked into Freya's face.

"I've got it!" she said at last. "You're the Birthday Girl – and you're stuck here for the Big Day. Is that right?"

"That's right," said Freya, crossly.

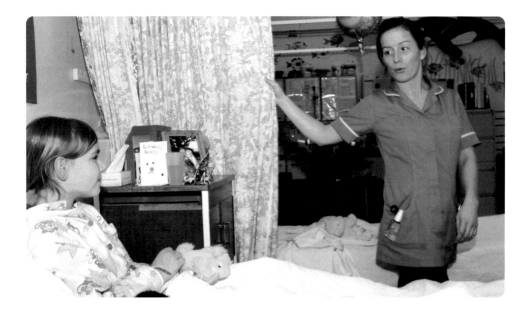

"What sort of party were you planning?" asked Leanne. "A movie? Swimming?"

"Bowling," said Freya, quietly, "with pizza afterward."

"Mmm," replied Leanne, shaking her head. "There's no way you're doing any bowling tomorrow."

"I know that!" snapped Leanne. "I'm trapped in this stupid bed!" She thumped the mattress hard.

"Hey!" said Leanne, gently. "Life doesn't stop just because you're in the hospital, you know. A birthday's a birthday — right?"

Freya shrugged. "What do you mean?"

"Wait and see!" grinned Leanne.

That afternoon, Leanne came back again. She got Freya ready for her operation and explained everything that was going on.

Soon Freya was being led to the anesthetic room. Her mom squeezed her hand as they walked along the corridor. All the time, Freya could hear Leanne humming in the background. It made things seem easier, somehow.

Later, Freya remembered someone calling her name. When she woke up properly, she was back in bed. It was nighttime. Her mom was sitting next to her, asleep in the chair.

Freya drifted off back to sleep.

Freya spent the morning with her mom, opening birthday cards and presents. Her mom gave her a karaoke machine, and there was a computer game and a sparkly jewelry box from her grandma and grandpa.

Freya heard Leanne's humming before she saw her. The tune was "Happy Birthday To You!" And she was pushing a trolley cart with plates of pizzas and chips. Tied to the cart was a bunch of balloons and behind Leanne, to Freya's amazement, were her three friends Tilly, Becky, and Elise.

"Party time, everyone!" called Leanne.

Lucy, the girl Freya had met in the playroom, came to join in. When it arrived, the birthday cake was big enough for them all to share. As Leanne carried it in, everyone sang.

Freya looked at Leanne and smiled.

Leanne winked. "What did I tell you?" she asked.

"A birthday's a birthday — wherever you are!"

Dear Aunt Jan,

Thanks for coming and bringing me the face paints. We had a good time with them.

I did what you said and told Mr. Green, the teacher here, about Sammie and Kim. We came up with the idea of writing an account of my stay here for everyone at school and illustrating it with photos. So I wrote all about my operation and what it's like being in hospital. Then I got a card from the whole class, and Sammie, Kim and some of the others came to visit me. Mrs. Barlow came too.

I go back to school after vacation. I'm looking forward to it. But I'll miss everyone here. I'll need to come back in six weeks' time to be checked. Louise the playworker says I can come in any time and help in the playroom.

Lots of love,

Grace xxx

Dear Grace,

Thank you for your letter and the crazy drawing of yourself! It's great. I've put it on my bulletin board.

I'm glad things have worked out so well for you and that you're looking forward to going back to school. After six weeks, you'll probably be really looking forward to going back to the hospital for your checkup. I expect you will find it strange to be an "outpatient," just visiting the hospital and not staying.

I'm sure your mom and dad will be pleased to have you home. Give them my love.

Lots of love,

Aunt Jan xx

Glossary

anesthetic (an-uhs-THET-ik)
A type of medicine that numbs a person's skin or body parts before an operation or medical test

emergency (e-MUR-juhn-see)
A serious, unexpected event that demands immediate action

hospital (HOS-pi-tuhl)
A place that treats sick or injured people, including people who may need surgery or long-term care

injection (in-JEK-shun)
A shot given by a nurse or doctor to put medicine into a person's body through a needle

operation (op-uh-RAY-shun)
A medical procedure performed by a surgeon to fix or improve a problem with a person's body

For Further Reading

Thomas, Pat. *Do I Have to Go to the Hospital?: A First Look at Going to the Hospital.* Barron's Educational Series, Inc., 2006.

Civardi, Anne. *Going to the Hospital.* EDC Publishing, 2005.

Web Sites

To find Web sites related to the subject of this book, please go to www.windmillbooks.com/weblinks and select this book's title.

Index

A
anesthetic 15, 21

C
children's ward 5, 10, 19, 24

E
emergency 17

F
feelings 14, 20
friends 12-13, 15-16

H
hospital 4, 12, 18-19

I
Injections 4, 15

O
operation 12, 21

S
school 12-13, 15-16, 23

X
X-ray 12

For more great fiction and nonfiction, go to windmillbooks.com.